ECDL® 5.0

European Computer Driving Licence

Module 7b - Communication

Using Microsoft® Outlook 2010

Release ECDL278v1

Published by:

CiA Training Ltd
Business & Innovation Centre
Sunderland Enterprise Park
Sunderland
SR5 2TA
United Kingdom   3 9 5 4 8 6 3   3·50

005·52

Tel: +44 (0) 191 549 5002
Fax: +44 (0) 191 549 9005

E-mail: info@ciatraining.co.uk
Web: www.ciatraining.co.uk

ISBN: 978-1-86005-857-8

Important Note

This guide was written for *Microsoft Office 2010* running on *Windows 7*. If using earlier versions of *Windows* some dialog boxes may look and function slightly differently to that described.

A screen resolution of *1024x768* is assumed. Working at a different resolution (or with an application window which is not maximised) may change the look of the dynamic *Office 2010 Ribbon*, which changes to fit the space available.

For example, the **Editing Group** on a full *Ribbon* will contain several buttons, but if space is restricted it may be replaced by an **Editing Button** (which, when clicked, will display the full **Editing Group**).

First published 2010

Copyright © 2010 CiA Training Ltd

European Computer Driving Licence, ECDL, International Computer Driving Licence, ICDL, e-Citizen and related logos are all registered Trade Marks of The European Computer Driving Licence Foundation Limited ("ECDL Foundation").

CiA Training Ltd is an entity independent of ECDL Foundation and is not associated with ECDL Foundation in any manner. This courseware may be used to assist candidates to prepare for the ECDL Foundation Certification Programme as titled on the courseware. Neither ECDL Foundation nor **CiA Training Ltd** warrants that the use of this courseware publication will ensure passing of the tests for that ECDL Foundation Certification Programme. This courseware publication has been independently reviewed and approved by ECDL Foundation as covering the learning objectives for the ECDL Foundation Certification Programme.

Confirmation of this approval can be obtained by viewing the relevant ECDL Foundation Certification Programme training material page of the website www.ecdl.org.

The material contained in this courseware publication has not been reviewed for technical accuracy and does not guarantee that candidates will pass the test for the ECDL Foundation Certification Programme. Any and all assessment items and/or performance-based exercises contained in this courseware relate solely to this publication and do not constitute or imply certification by ECDL Foundation in respect of the ECDL Foundation Certification Programme or any other ECDL Foundation test. Irrespective of how the material contained in this courseware is deployed, for example in a learning management system (LMS) or a customised interface, nothing should suggest to the candidate that this material constitutes certification or can lead to certification through any other process than official ECDL Foundation certification testing.

For details on sitting a test for an ECDL Foundation certification programme, please contact your country's designated National Licensee or visit the ECDL Foundation's website at www.ecdl.org.

Candidates using this courseware must be registered with the National Operator before undertaking a test for an ECDL Foundation Certification Programme. Without a valid registration, the test(s) cannot be undertaken and no certificate, nor any other form of recognition, can be given to a candidate. Registration should be undertaken with your country's designated National Licensee at an Approved Test Centre.

ECDL Foundation
Approved Courseware

Downloading the Data Files

The data files associated with these exercises must be downloaded from our website. Go to *www.ciatraining.co.uk/data* and follow the on screen instructions to download the appropriate data files.

By default, the data files will be installed to **CIA DATA FILES \ ECDL \ 7 Communications** in your **Documents** library\folder (or **My Documents** in *Windows XP*).

If you prefer, the data can be supplied on CD at an additional cost. Contact the Sales team at *info@ciatraining.co.uk*.

Aims

To demonstrate the ability to use an e-mail application on a personal computer. To create and send e-mail and to manage personal Contact Groups and message folders.

Objectives

After completing the guide the user will be able to:

- Understand what e-mail is and know some advantages and disadvantages of its use. Be aware of other communication options; be aware of network etiquette and security considerations when using e-mail

- Create, spell check and send e-mail. Reply to and forward e-mail, handle file attachments and print an e-mail

- Be aware of ways to enhance productivity when working with e-mail software. Organise and manage e-mail

Assessment of Knowledge

At the end of this guide is a section called the **Record of Achievement Matrix**. Before the guide is started it is recommended that the user complete the matrix to measure the level of current knowledge.

Tick boxes are provided for each feature. **1** is for no knowledge, **2** some knowledge and **3** is for competent.

After working through a section, complete the **Record of Achievement** matrix for that section and only when competent in all areas move on to the next section.

Contents

Section 1
Outlook

By the end of this Section you should be able to:

Understand Electronic Messaging and Related Issues

Use Online Help

Change Views

Sort Messages

Close Outlook

To gain an understanding of the above features, work through the **Driving Lessons** in this **Section**.

For each **Driving Lesson**, read the **Park and Read** instructions, without touching the keyboard, then work through the numbered steps of the **Manoeuvres** on the computer. Complete the **Revision Exercise(s)** at the end of the section to test your knowledge.

Driving Lesson 1 - Using E-mail

▣ Park and Read

Today, e-mail is an extremely important and efficient communication tool and many businesses would come to a standstill without it. It has obvious advantages over the normal postal system: it is much faster – mail is delivered within seconds. Rather than pay postage costs for sending paper copies of files through the post or by courier, electronic files can simply be attached to e-mail messages. Consider how much more quickly business documents can be sent overseas using e-mail rather than by using surface or airmail. A point of note is that some anti-virus software/firewalls may prevent certain types of attachment from being sent via e-mail (this is because some viruses are spread by being attached to e-mail messages).

Before using e-mail, try to familiarise yourself with the rules of **netiquette** - network etiquette. Always be accurate and keep your messages brief and as relevant as possible, and don't forget to include a short subject. Avoid sending heated, angry messages (known as **flames**) and don't use all UPPERCASE words – this is the same as shouting. Make sure your messages are spelled correctly, just as you would for a real letter, and be careful not to overdo your use of colours and fonts.

Consider the implications very carefully before sending any sensitive information by e-mail. In a work situation, you must familiarise yourself with the e-mail policy in place. Usually, common business rules and regulations state that you must not circulate inappropriate or offensive messages (including jokes and "chain mail"). Basically, only subject matter directly associated with the business should be sent via e-mail.

Unwanted Messages

Be prepared to receive unwanted e-mail (known as **spam**). Certain companies and individuals send out a lot of such junk mail, often in an attempt to sell you something. Of course, you can simply delete these e-mails as you would throw away real unwanted mail (*Outlook* can even be set up to do this automatically for you). Many of these types of messages also have a means to allow you to **unsubscribe** from their **mailing list**, so no further messages will be sent to you. It is always worth scanning the message for this.

Identity theft is also a risk with e-mail. Be suspicious of any e-mail from people you do not know, and be very careful about acting on any instructions given in them (for example, opening attached files or installing special software to remove viruses). Any message which promises riches, prizes, or rewards should be regarded with the suspicion they deserve and be deleted <u>immediately</u>. In particular, banks will <u>never</u> ask for account information or passwords/PINs to be put in an e-mail, no matter how official the requesting e-mail may appear to be. This technique is used by fraudsters to get access to your accounts, and is known as **phishing.** If in doubt, it is a good idea to get a second opinion from an experienced person whose opinion you trust.

continued over

Driving Lesson 1 - Continued

One way to be certain of the authenticity of an e-mail is to use a **digital signature**. Although rarely used in typical communications, this technique guarantees that the recipient of an e-mail (or any other file) can be certain of the sender's identity. The recipient can also be confident that the contents of the message are complete and have not been tampered with in any way. Furthermore, if you **encrypt** (scramble) the message, it's very difficult for anyone other than the intended recipient to even read the e-mail.

As described earlier, always be vigilant about e-mail messages with attachments – even those from friends – as they can potentially contain viruses. Ensure you have antivirus software installed on your computer and keep it up-to-date by allowing it to automatically download updates. Messages without a subject or from an unknown source should be treated with caution. As a rule, always save attached files to disk and scan them with your antivirus software before opening. If you do open a message attachment that contains a virus, the results can be disastrous for your computer (and possibly the other computers on your network).

Web-based E-mail

As well as installing a program such as *Outlook* on your computer to manage your e-mail, it is possible to set up an e-mail account that is **web based**. Messages can be collected and sent from any computer with an Internet connection, anywhere in the world. After setting up your account, it's a simple matter of logging on to send or receive your messages. One disadvantage of web based accounts, however, is that disk space is limited, which means that you need to keep an eye on the size of messages in your mailbox.

Driving Lesson 2 - Using Outlook

▣ Park and Read

For many people who are connected to the Internet, a large amount of their online time is spent sending and receiving e-mail messages. *Microsoft Outlook 2010* is an application that lets you do this – it can be used to manage all electronic messages coming to and going from your computer. E-mails can be easily composed and sent anywhere in the world, and files can be attached to a message in a couple of simple steps.

You can also use *Outlook* as a **personal information manager**. The **Contacts** facility stores information about people you know, and the powerful **Calendar** and **Tasks** features allow you to keep track of appointments, meetings and to-do lists. *Outlook* can also receive **Newsgroup** and **RSS/News Feeds** – summarised messages from news websites that you have subscribed to.

Before you can fully use *Outlook*, however, you will need an **e-mail address**. Very simply, an address takes the form **username@domain**, where:

username -	is the name of the recipient of the e-mail (usually your name)
@ sign -	separates the username from the domain name.
domain -	is the name of a computer which sends and receives mail (your organisation or internet service provider).

Microsoft Outlook 2010 is supplied as part of *Microsoft Office 2010*. Of note, when you are not using *Outlook*, messages are stored for you until they are collected. You do not need to keep the program running all of the time.

⌐ Manoeuvres

1. Click once on the **Start** button, (situated at the bottom left of the screen, on the **Taskbar**), to show the list of start options available. All *Windows* applications can be started from here.

2. Move the mouse pointer to **All Programs**.

3. Click the **Microsoft Office** folder to display its contents and then click **Microsoft Outlook 2010**. Alternatively there may be icons to start *Outlook* on the **Start Menu** itself, on the **Desktop**, or on the **Taskbar**.

4. After a moment, the *Outlook* window will be displayed.

continued over

Driving Lesson 2 - Continued

i *Outlook must be configured before it can be used for the first time. Configuring is the term used to describe the supply of user information to the program. If the Internet Connection Wizard or Add New Account dialog appears when you start Outlook, contact your IT Administrator or Internet Service Provider who will be able to help you configure the program.*

i *When you start Outlook you may first be asked to connect to the internet – you need to do this to send and receive e-mail. Also, if there is more than one e-mail profile available on the computer, you will need to select one.*

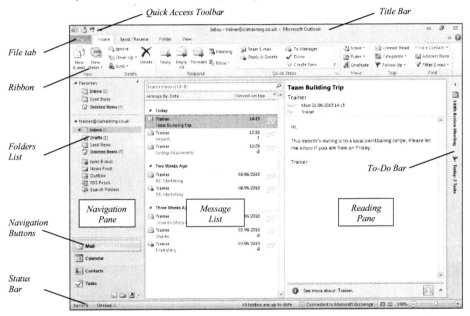

5. If the **Inbox** is not currently selected (and its contents displayed in the **Message List**), select it now by clicking **Inbox** from the **Folders List** on the **Navigation Pane**.

i *The screen may not look exactly like this as there are many display options available. Depending on your mailbox type, the **Quick Steps** group may be smaller and an extra **Send/Receive** group may appear on the **Ribbon**. This picture shows the **Navigation Pane, Message List** and **Reading Pane**. The **Mail** button is selected and the **To-Do Bar** is minimized.*

i *Depending on your configuration, you may see more than one mailbox in the **Folders List**. If this is the case, you have more than one e-mail account set up in Outlook, and each will have its own collection of folders (i.e. **Inbox, Sent Items**, etc). For this guide, use the folders within the mailbox that has your main e-mail address as its title, e.g.* ◢ Trainer@ciatraining.co.uk .

continued over

Driving Lesson 2 - Continued

6. Locate and familiarise yourself with all the features shown on the previous page.

7. The **Title Bar** is at the top of the *Outlook* screen. It shows the application and the name of the mailbox that is currently open.

8. At the top left of the screen is the **Quick Access Toolbar,** . By default this contains two buttons, **Send/Receive All Folders** and **Undo**. More buttons can be added to this toolbar.

9. Under this toolbar is an area called the **Ribbon**. This consists of a range of **tabs** containing buttons within groups.

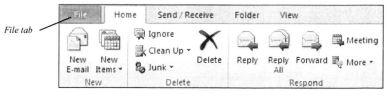

File tab

ℹ️ *The **File** tab contains a list of basic program functions such as **Open**, **Save As**, **Print** and **Exit**. More advanced options can also be found here.*

10. The buttons on the **Ribbon** are used to select an action or command in *Outlook*. Move the cursor over any button but do not click. Read the **ToolTip** that appears which gives the name of that button and a small description, e.g. **New E-mail** in the **New** group on the **Home** tab.

11. The **Status Bar** runs along the bottom of the window. This displays messages as tasks are performed. It will currently show the total number of messages (or *items*) in your **Inbox**.

12. The right side of the **Status Bar** contains a set of **Views** buttons and a **Zoom** slider.

13. Leave the *Outlook* window open for the next Driving Lesson.

Driving Lesson 3 - Help

Park and Read

Outlook has a comprehensive **Help** facility. This means that full advantage can be taken of the features incorporated in the program. Using **Help** can usually solve the majority of problems encountered.

Help topics are available either from **Office.com** (via the internet) or from the content installed on your computer (offline). The method of using **Help** is the same in either case but the content may vary slightly.

Manoeuvres

1.   Click the **Help** button, 📷, in the upper right corner of the *Outlook* window, to display the **Outlook Help** window.

ℹ️   *Pressing the <F1> key will display the same **Help** window. The window can be moved, resized or maximised if required.*

2.   If the **Table of Contents** panel is not displayed on the left, as shown below, click the **Show Table of Contents** button, 📷, on the **Help** toolbar.

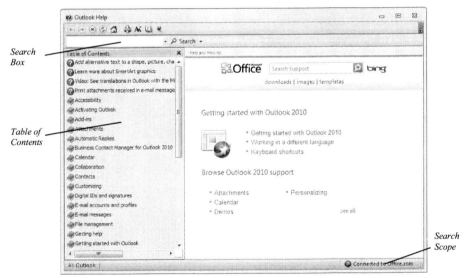

3.   The **Search Scope** button at the bottom of the window indicates whether you are connected to **Office.com** or not (offline). Click on the button to see the available options, and make sure **Show content from Office.com** is selected.

continued over

Driving Lesson 3 - Continued

i *The content and appearance of the information provided by the online Help system will change over time and may not be exactly as described here.*

4. **Help** can be used in two ways. You can either browse through the listed topics or type keywords into the **Search** box.

5. A list of categories is shown on the opening screen in the main display area. Click on any one that interests you to display a list of relevant hyperlinked topics.

6. Scan the topics shown and click any that are of interest.

i *The same information can be found using by navigating the Table of Contents.*

7. To move back to a previous screen, click the **Back** button, on the dialog box toolbar. You can then follow another link.

i *Help topics can be printed for reference by clicking the Print button,*

8. Click the **Home** button, on the dialog box toolbar to return directly to the starting help screen.

9. Another way to find help is to search by keyword. Type **shortcuts** into the **Search** box and click the **Search** button,

> ## Search results for: **shortcuts**
>
> Keyboard **shortcuts** for Clip Organizer
>   Article | Toolbar shortcuts To do this Press Display the Collection List task pa...
>
> Keyboard **shortcuts** in Business Contact Manager
>   Article | A keyboard shortcut is any combination of keystrokes that can be us...
>
> Accessibility Features in Microsoft Office 2010
>   Article | Microsoft Office 2010 continues the dedication to both making Micr...

i *There may be many topics found for your search and it will be necessary for you to use your own judgement and select the most appropriate one.*

10. Click the **Home** button, to return to the starting screen.

i *The Table of Contents can be hidden by clicking the Hide Table of Contents button,* *, on the Help toolbar.*

11. Close the **Help** window by clicking its **Close** button,

Driving Lesson 4 - Views

🅿 Park and Read

By default, when *Outlook* starts, it will show a **Folders List** containing a number of mailbox folders, e.g. **Inbox**, **Sent Items**, etc. The display, or **view**, changes depending on the folder (or **Navigation Button**) selected.

👣 Manoeuvres

1. If the **Inbox** is not selected on the **Navigation Pane**, select it now by clicking **Inbox** from the **Folders List** (make sure the **Navigation Button** *Mail* is selected first).

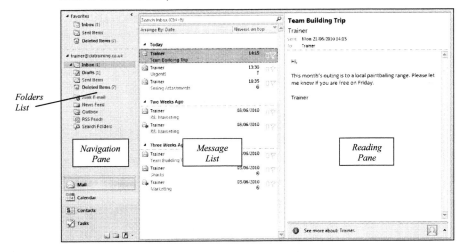

ℹ️ *The layout of this screen may vary. The example above shows the **Navigation Pane**, the **Message List** and the **Reading Pane**.*

2. Look at the **Message List** which shows messages you have received. Messages in **bold** type have not been read yet (and show a closed envelope icon, ✉). Messages which are <u>not</u> bold have been read (and show an open envelope icon, ✉).

3. Select any message from the **Message List** (if there are any) and its contents are previewed in the **Reading Pane**.

4. If you'd rather not automatically preview messages, the **Reading Pane** can be hidden. Display the **View** tab and click the **Reading Pane** button in the **Layout** group. Select the **Off** option.

continued over

Driving Lesson 4 - Continued

5.   To turn the **Reading Pane** back on, click the **Reading Pane** button again and select the **Right** option (**Bottom** places the **Reading Pane** below the **Message List**).

ℹ️ *Similar options are available to hide/show the **Navigation Pane** and the **To-Do Bar**. The widths of the **Navigation Pane, Message List, Reading Pane** and **To-Do Bar** can be adjusted by clicking and dragging the boundary line between them.*

6.   To expand the **To-Do Bar**, click the **To-Do Bar** button and select **Normal**. The **To-Do Bar** shows upcoming appointments and tasks listed in the **Calendar** and **Tasks** views.

7.   Click the **Minimize the To-Do Bar** button, 📙, at the top left of the **To-Do Bar**, to hide it again.

8.   To minimise the **Ribbon**, click the **Minimize the Ribbon** button, ⌃, shown at the top right of the *Outlook* window (or press **<Ctrl F1>**). Hiding the **Ribbon** gives you a little more room to work in.

9.   To restore the **Ribbon**, click the **Expand the Ribbon** button, ⌄.

10. Click the **Calendar** button on the **Navigation Pane**. The *Outlook* **Calendar** is shown. This can be used to plan your daily activities and to schedule appointments and meetings.

ℹ️ *If your organisation supports it, you can choose to share your **Calendar** with others on your network. This makes it very easy for others to see what you are doing and to organise meetings with your colleagues.*

11. Click the **Tasks** button on the **Navigation Pane**. This view can be used to create task lists and reminders.

✓ Tasks

ℹ️ *Upcoming **Calendar** and **Tasks** items for today appear on the **To-Do Bar**.*

12. Click the **Mail** button on the **Navigation Pane** to return to your mailbox.

ℹ️ ***Calendar** and **Tasks** aren't covered in detail in this guide as they are not included in the ECDL syllabus.*

Driving Lesson 5 - Sorting Messages

P Park and Read

The headings in the **Message List** can be used to sort the information that is shown. For example, you can rearrange messages alphabetically by subject or sender, or by size or the date received.

Manoeuvres

1. Turn off the **Reading Pane** by displaying the **View** tab and clicking the **Reading Pane** button and then selecting the option **Off**. The **Message List** expands to show information displayed in columns.

Reading Pane ▾

! △ ⃞ ⋃ From	Subject	Received ▼	Size	Categories ▽ ▲
◢ Date: Yesterday				
⁂ Trainer	Team Building Trip	Wed 10/02/2010 11:39	6 KB	▽
◢ Date: Last Week				
▷ ⃝ ⋃ Terry Charlton; Trainer	Appointment	Thu 04/02/2010 18:07	15 KB	▽
⁂ Bob Browell	Urgent	Thu 04/02/2010 18:06	5 KB	▽
⋃ Trainer	Dinner Arrangements	Wed 03/02/2010 11:11	9 KB	▽

ℹ *Depending on the width of the **Message List**, messages in your mailbox may already be displayed in columns. However, if there is not enough space, the **Message List** will display a more compact view instead.*

2. The way in which this information is displayed can be easily changed. By default, messages are sorted in date order, with the newest at the top. Click the header titled **Received**; messages are now sorted in reverse order, with the oldest at the top.

From	Subject	Received ▲	Size

ℹ *Notice that the downwards arrow icon on the header, ▼, has changed to point upwards indicating the sort has been reversed.*

3. Click the **Size** header to sort the messages by their file size. Click the **Size** header again to reverse the sort.

4. Click the **From** header to sort messages alphabetically by the name of their sender. Click **From** again to reverse the sort.

5. Click the **Received** header again to restore the sort to newest items first.

ℹ *You can click any of the column headers to sort messages in your mailbox. A second click reverses that ordering.*

continued over

Driving Lesson 5 - Continued

6. You can also add and remove columns. Display the **View** tab and click the **Add Columns** button, in the **Arrangement** group.

7. The **Show Columns** dialog appears showing all the available columns that can be used on the left. The list on the right shows the columns currently displayed. Compare it with the first picture in this driving lesson.

8. Click **Categories** from the list on the right, and then click the **Remove** button. The column is removed from the list and appears back on the left.

9. Click on **Cc** from the list on the left and then click the **Add** button. The column is added to the bottom of the list on the right.

10. With the **Cc** column item still selected in the rightmost list, click the **Move Up** button until the item is positioned between **Subject** and **Received**.

11. Click **OK**. The new column headings are shown in the **Message List**. Notice that **Cc** has now appeared and **Categories** has disappeared.

> The width of individual columns can be varied by clicking and dragging the column boundaries on the header row.

12. To replace the headings in their original locations, display the **View** tab and click the **Reset View** button in the **Current View** group. Click **Yes** to confirm the action.

> If the **Reading Pane** has not reappeared, turn it on again by displaying the **View** tab and clicking the **Reading Pane** button, and then selecting **Right**.

Driving Lesson 6 - Closing Outlook

▣ Park and Read

Outlook can be closed at any time. In some instances you may need to terminate your *Internet* connection also, if no prompt to disconnect appears automatically (for example, if you are on a dial-up connection).

When *Outlook* is not running, incoming messages will continue to be received and held, either by your Internet Service Provider or your organisation's server. When you next connect, all waiting messages will be passed to your mailbox.

↱ Manoeuvres

1.   Click the **Close** button on the **Title Bar** at the top right of the screen.

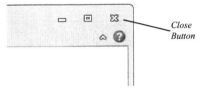

Close Button

i *Alternatively, select* **Exit** *from the* **File** *tab.*

2.   If you have a dial-up connection the **Auto Disconnect** dialog box should appear. Select **Disconnect Now** if you wish to end the current session.

i *You may need to disconnect a dial-up connection manually if no prompt to do so appears automatically.*

Driving Lesson 7 - Revision

This covers the features introduced in this section. Try not to refer to the preceding Driving Lessons while completing it.

1. List some advantages of using e-mail in a business environment.

2. What is netiquette?

3. What can gain access to your computer via e-mail messages?

4. What can you do to protect your computer?

5. What is e-mail?

6. What are the three sections of an e-mail address?

7. Start *Outlook*.

8. Hide the **Ribbon** and the **Reading Pane**.

9. Restore the **Ribbon** and the **Reading Pane**.

10. View the **Show Columns** dialog box which allows the mailbox columns to be changed.

11. View only the following columns in the order stated: **Attachment, Flag Status, Importance, From, Received, Subject**.

12. Reset the view to its original state.

13. Close *Outlook*.

[i] *Answers are shown in the **Answers** section at the end of this guide.*

If you experienced any difficulty completing the Revision, refer back to the Driving Lessons in this section. Then redo the Revision.

Once you are confident with the features, complete the Record of Achievement Matrix referring to the section at the end of the guide. Only when competent move on to the next Section.

Section 2
Message Editing

By the end of this Section you should be able to:

Create a Message

Insert and Delete Text

Cut, Copy and Paste Messages

Copy and Paste from Word

Use the Spell Checker

Add an AutoSignature to a Message

To gain an understanding of the above features, work through the **Driving Lessons** in this **Section**.

For each **Driving Lesson**, read the **Park and Read** instructions, without touching the keyboard, then work through the numbered steps of the **Manoeuvres** on the computer. Complete the **Revision Exercise(s)** at the end of the section to test your knowledge.

Driving Lesson 8 - Creating a Message

P Park and Read

Outlook allows the user to send an e-mail message to anyone on the Internet, as long as the recipient's e-mail address is known.

Manoeuvres

1. Start *Outlook* and make sure the **Home** tab is displayed on the **Ribbon**.

2. Click the **New E-mail** button. An **Untitled Message** window is displayed with the **Message** tab selected in the **Ribbon** area.

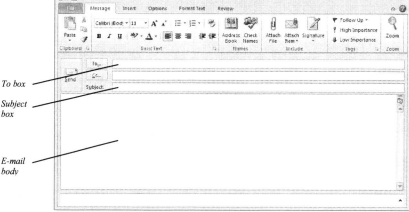

i *You can maximise the **Message** window to see more of the **Ribbon** by clicking the **Maximize** button, on the window's **Title Bar**.*

3. The **Ribbon** can be minimized to display more space for the message. Click on the **Minimize the Ribbon** button, .

4. Notice that the **Ribbon** headers remain visible. Click **Message** and the **Message** tab is temporarily displayed. Click away from the **Ribbon** and it is minimized again. Click the **Expand the Ribbon** button, , to restore the **Ribbon**.

5. Type your own e-mail address in the **To** box.

6. In the **Subject** box, enter **Sending messages**.

continued over

Driving Lesson 8 - Continued

7. Type the following text into the main message area of the window, also known as the **e-mail body**:

    Always remember to check your e-mail regularly

8. Double click on the word **regularly** to select it, and then press **<Delete>**. Insert the new text: **at regular intervals throughout the day!**

i *Methods for inserting, deleting and formatting text in Outlook are the same as in most word processing packages.*

9. Press **<Enter>** to start a new line and type: **You don't want to miss important messages**.

10. Select the two sentences. You are going to change their formatting. Make sure both sentences remain selected as each of the following effects are applied.

11. Look at the **Basic Text** group of buttons on the **Message** tab. Click on the **Font** drop down arrow, | Calibri (Body) ▾ |, and select **Comic Sans MS**.

12. With the text still highlighted, use the **Font Size** button, | 11 ▾ |, to change the text to **12pt** and embolden the text by clicking the **Bold** button, **B**.

13. Change the text to bulleted points by clicking **Bullets**, | ☰ ▾ |.

14. Indent the bulleted list to the right by clicking **Increase Indent**, | ⇥ |.

15. Click **Decrease Indent**, | ⇤ |, to restore the bullets to their original positions.

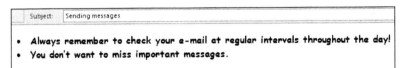

| Subject: | Sending messages |

- Always remember to check your e-mail at regular intervals throughout the day!
- You don't want to miss important messages.

16. Use the alignment buttons, | ≡ ≡ ≡ |, to see the effect of changing the layout of the text.

17. Finally make sure the text is left aligned.

18. Leave the message open for the next Driving Lesson.

Driving Lesson 9 - Cut, Copy and Paste Messages

▣ Park and Read

It is possible to cut, copy and paste text to a different location within a message or to a different message entirely.

↱ Manoeuvres

1.   With the **Sending messages** e-mail still open from the previous Driving Lesson, use click and drag to select all the text in the e-mail body.

2.   From the **Message** tab, click **Copy**, 🗐, or press **<Ctrl C>**. The original text is left in the message, but a copy of it is now invisibly written to a temporary area of storage called the **Clipboard**.

3.   Position the cursor at the end of the text, and then press **<Enter>** to create a new line.

4.   Click the **Paste** button from the **Message** tab or press **<Ctrl V>** to paste the copied text from the **Clipboard** into the message at the point where the cursor is flashing.

ⓘ   *Cut or copied text remains on the **Clipboard** until another item is cut or copied. It can be pasted as many times as you like.*

5.   Now select the first sentence and click **Cut**, ✄, or press **<Ctrl X>**. The text is removed from the message to the **Clipboard**.

6.   Position the cursor at the end of the text and click the **Paste** button to paste in the cut text.

7.   Minimise the message window to display the main *Outlook* window. Click the **New E-Mail** button again to start a new message, and enter **Pasting** in the **Subject** box.

8.   Click in the e-mail body and click the **Paste** button again. The text from the first message (**Sending messages**) is pasted into the new message.

9.   Click the **Sending messages** button on the **Taskbar** to redisplay the first message.

10. At the end of the message type **Regards** and then your name. Copy this new text and use the **Taskbar** to return to the **Pasting** message.

11. Paste in the copied text at the end of the **Pasting** message.

12. Close the **Pasting** message by clicking the **Close** button, ⊠, at the top right of its **Title Bar**. Select **No** if a prompt to save appears.

13. Click **Send** to send the **Sending messages** e-mail.

Driving Lesson 10 - Copy and Paste from Word

▣ Park and Read

It is possible to cut or copy text from a *Word* document and paste it into an e-mail message, so that time is not spent re-entering the same text. If the entire document was to be used in the message, it is more usual to attach the file. This will be discussed in **Section 3**.

⌐ Manoeuvres

1. Close *Outlook*, then start *Word* (**Start | All Programs | Microsoft Office | Microsoft Word 2010**).

2. Type in the following text:

   **To save myself time, I can use existing text in my
   Outlook messages.**

3. Select the text and click the **Copy** button, 🖻, to copy the text to your **Clipboard** (or press **<Ctrl C>**).

4. Click the **File** tab, █File█, and select **Exit**, ☒ Exit, to close *Word*. Do not save any changes if prompted.

5. Open *Outlook* and start a new message.

6. Enter your own e-mail address in the **To** box.

7. Enter the subject: **Pasting from Word**.

8. Click within the **E-mail body** to place the cursor and either click the **Paste** button or press **<Ctrl V>** to paste the text created in *Word*.

9. If necessary, insert a space at the end of the text and type:

   This text has been pasted from a word processing application.

10. Click and drag to select the text: **a word processing application**.

11. This text is to be deleted. Press **<Delete>** to remove it.

12. Replace the deleted text with the new text: **Microsoft Word**.

    > To save myself time, I can use existing text in my Outlook messages. This text has been pasted from Microsoft Word.|

13. Click **Send** to send the message, and leave *Outlook* open for the next lesson.

Driving Lesson 11 - Spell Checker

▣ Park and Read

Outlook contains a spell-checking feature which can be used to check the spelling in messages before they are sent. The spell checker is very similar to the one available in *Microsoft Word*.

↱ Manoeuvres

1. Create a new message with intentional spelling mistakes, similar to the one shown below.

ℹ️ *The option to underline spelling mistakes in red as you enter the text (as seen in the picture above) is described later in this lesson. Some simple spelling mistakes may also be corrected automatically as you type.*

2. Display the **Review** tab and click the **Spelling & Grammar** button in the **Proofing** group. The **Spelling and Grammar** dialog box appears, highlighting the first word that the spell checker does not recognise, i.e. "wunder".

continued over

Driving Lesson 11 - Continued

3.   There are options to leave the word as it is (**Ignore Once/All**) or **Change** it. Select the correct choice from the **Suggestions** list (wonder) and click **Change**.

4.   The word is changed in the message and the spell checker moves on to the next unknown word, i.e. "gud".

5.   Continue to correct the remaining errors as they are found, either by changing or ignoring them.

6.   The spell checker will also find duplicated words – if any are found, click the **Delete** button in the dialog box to remove one of the duplications.

7.   Click **OK** when the message appears to say the check is complete.

i *In general, the spell checker only highlights as spelling mistakes words that are not in its dictionary. For example, the words **weak** and **allot** are both incorrect in our example, but because they are valid words, they may not be marked as spelling mistakes.*

8.   From the main *Outlook* window, display the **File** tab, [File], and select **Options**.

9.   Select **Mail** from the category list on the left.

10.   There is an option shown in **Compose messages** to **Always check spelling before sending**. Check this option if you want all messages to be spell-checked automatically before being sent.

11.   Also in **Compose messages**, click the **Spelling and Autocorrect** button. Examine all the options which control how the spell checker works.

12.   There is an option to **Check spelling as you type**. Check this option if you want spelling mistakes to be highlighted (with red underline) as you are entering text.

> When correcting spelling in Outlook
>
> ☑ Check spelling as you type
> ☑ Use contextual spelling

i *The **Use contextual spelling** option will help to find words that are spelled correctly but used improperly, such as **weak** and **allot** in our example.*

13.   Click **OK** to close the **Editor Options** dialog box, and then **OK** again to close the main **Outlook Options** dialog box.

14.   Close the e-mail message window <u>without</u> saving, but leave *Outlook* open for the next exercise.

Driving Lesson 12 - Applying a Signature

▣ Park and Read

A personal signature can be added to the end of e-mail messages automatically, without the need to type it each time. You can set up any number of signatures in *Outlook* and can easily select the most appropriate one for the message you are composing.

⟲ Manoeuvres

1. To create a signature, display the **File** tab from the main *Outlook* window, and select **Options**. Select **Mail** from the list on the left. In **Compose messages** there is an option to maintain signatures.

2. Click the **Signatures** button.

3. Click the **New** button. Enter **Full Title** as the name of your signature to help you identify it, and then click **OK**.

4. In the large **Edit signature** box, enter your name and, on the next line, a job title and department (or company name). For example:

> **Kate Jones**
> **Financial Controller**
> **Midlands Division**

continued over

Driving Lesson 12 - Continued

5.   Highlight your name and click the drop down arrow on the **Font** box,
      | Calibri (Body) ▼ |.

6.   Scroll down the list of fonts and select **Freestyle Script** (or similar to that
      shown below) and a **Size** of **24**.

> Edi̱t signature
>
> | Freestyle Script ▼ | 24 ▼ |
>
> *Kate Jones*
>
> Financial Controller
> Midlands Division

7.   To add this signature automatically to all new messages, click the drop
      down arrow in the **New Messages** box (under **Choose default
      signature**) and select **Full Title**.

> Choose default signature
>
> | E-mail a̱ccount: | Microsoft Exchange | ▼ |
> | New m̱essages: | Full Title | ▼ |
> | Replies/f̱orwards: | (none) | ▼ |

8.   Click **OK**, then **OK** again to close the dialog boxes.

ℹ️ *Several signatures can be added in this way to cover various situations.*

9.   Start a new message. The signature automatically appears in the e-mail
      body. Highlight the signature text and delete it.

10.   To add a signature manually, display the **Insert** tab on the
      Ribbon and click the **Signature** button from the **Include** group.
      A list of all available signatures is shown. Select **Full Title** and it
      will appear in the message again.

11.   Close the message <u>without</u> saving.

12.   To stop the signature appearing automatically, display the **File** tab from
      the main *Outlook* window and select **Options**. Select **Mail** from the list of
      categories on the left and click the **Signatures** button again. Drop down
      the list for **New messages** and select **(none)**.

13.   To delete a signature altogether, select it from the **Select signature to
      edit** list on the left of the dialog box and click the **Delete** button. Click **Yes**
      to confirm the action.

14.   Click **OK** and **OK** again to close the dialog boxes.

Driving Lesson 13 - Revision

This covers the features introduced in this section. Try not to refer to the preceding Driving Lessons while completing it.

1. Compose a new message and address it to a friend.

2. Enter the subject as **Holiday**.

3. Enter the following message:

    Hi,

    I've just heard that you're going on holiday to Egypt and will be visiting the Valley of the Kings. Here's something that may interest you.

    Enjoy your holiday.

4. Press <**Enter**> and open *Word*. Open the **Kingtut** file from the data files folder.

5. Copy the first four paragraphs, then close *Word* <u>without</u> saving.

6. Paste the text into the e-mail message.

7. Delete the following text: **the "boy king", as he is often called,**.

8. Cut **Enjoy your holiday.** from the original message text and paste it at the end of the message after the imported text.

9. Spell check the message.

10. Close the message <u>without</u> saving.

If you experienced any difficulty completing the Revision, refer back to the Driving Lessons in this section. Then redo the Revision.

Driving Lesson 14 - Revision

This covers the features introduced in this section. Try not to refer to the preceding Driving Lessons while completing it.

1.   Start a new message.

2.   Address it to a friend.

3.   The subject is **Viruses**.

4.   Enter this message:

> **I thought I should warn you that e-mail messages can contain viruses. Make sure your antivirus software is up-to-date.**

5.   Create an informal signature for yourself.

6.   Add it to the message.

7.   Close the message <u>without</u> saving.

8.   Delete your signature from the **Options** dialog box.

If you experienced any difficulty completing the Revision, refer back to the Driving Lessons in this section. Then redo the Revision.

Once you are confident with the features, complete the Record of Achievement Matrix referring to the section at the end of the guide. Only when competent move on to the next Section.

Section 3
Send and Receive

By the end of this Section you should be able to:

Send, Open, Read and Flag Messages

Attach Files

Change Message Importance

Reply to and Forward Messages

Use Contacts

Add Sender to Contacts

Create and Use a Contact Group

To gain an understanding of the above features, work through the **Driving Lessons** in this **Section**.

For each **Driving Lesson**, read the **Park and Read** instructions, without touching the keyboard, then work through the numbered steps of the **Manoeuvres** on the computer. Complete the **Revision Exercise(s)** at the end of the section to test your knowledge.

Driving Lesson 15 - Sending Messages

▣ Park and Read

Outlook allows you to send messages to anyone on the Internet, so long as you know their e-mail address.

⟲ Manoeuvres

1. Click the **New E-mail** button to start a new message.

2. Enter your own e-mail address in the **To** box, so the message will come back to you and the results of this Driving Lesson can be observed.

3. In the **Subject** box, enter **Test message**.

4. A **carbon copy** of this message can be sent to another recipient who needs to take some action on it. Click in the **Cc** box and type in the e-mail address of a friend.

5. To send a copy of the message to someone without those in the **To** and **Cc** boxes knowing about, you can use the **Bcc** box which stands for **blind carbon copy**. To make this box available, display the **Options** tab and click **Bcc** from the **Show Fields** group. Enter a friend's e-mail address in the **Bcc** field (different to the one used in the previous step).

6. Type the following message text into the e-mail body:

    E-mail can be used to catch up with your friends, wherever they are, for free!

7. Click the **Send** button to send the message to the **Outbox**, ready to be sent. The message will usually be sent from here automatically by *Outlook* after a few moments.

ℹ️ *Outlook can be configured to only send and receive messages when told to do so. If this is the case, the message will stay in your **Outbox** until you click the **Send/Receive** button on the **Send/Receive** tab. When this button is clicked, Outlook also checks for any incoming mail.*

8. When the message has been sent, click on the **Sent Items** folder in the **Folders List**. A copy of all sent messages is kept here.

ℹ️ *The options to send messages immediately and save copies in the **Sent Items** folder can be set by displaying the **File** tab and selecting **Options | Advanced | Send and receive** or **Options | Mail | Save messages** respectively.*

9. It can sometimes take a few minutes for messages to be sent or received. Check with your friends that they received their copies of your message.

Driving Lesson 16 - Open and Read Messages

▣ Park and Read

Received e-mails are placed in the **Inbox** and are shown in bold type in the **Message List**, with an unopened envelope icon, ✉, next to the message's subject and sender's name. Once a message has been read, its icon changes to an opened envelope, ✉.

⎘ Manoeuvres

1. Display the **Send/Receive** tab and click the **Send/Receive All Folders** button. *Outlook* will check for new messages.

2. Make sure the **Mail** button is selected on the **Navigation Pane** and select **Inbox** from the **Folders List**. New messages will appear in the **Message List**; there should be at least one message present (**Test message**, which you sent to yourself earlier).

ⓘ *If the message has not arrived yet, wait for a few minutes and try **Send and Receive** again.*

3. To read a message in the **Message List**, click on it once and view its contents in the **Reading Pane** (you can also double click to open the message in a new window). Click once on the **Test message** and read its contents in the **Reading Pane**.

4. By default, the message will be marked as read as soon as another message or view is selected, but this can be changed. Display the **View** tab and click the **Reading Pane** button from the **Layout** group.

    [icon: Reading Pane ▾]

5. Select **Options**. The default settings are shown. Selecting **Mark items as read when viewed in the Reading Pane** and setting a **Wait** time will change the way messages are marked as read. Click **Cancel** to leave the setting unchanged.

    Reading Pane options
    ☐ Mark items as read when viewed in the Reading Pane
    Wait 5 seconds before marking item as read
    ☑ Mark item as read when selection changes
    ☑ Single key reading using space bar

    [OK] [Cancel]

6. To mark the selected **Test message** as **Unread**, display the **Home** tab and then click the **Unread/Read** button, [✉ Unread/Read], in the **Tags** group. The envelope icon changes back to closed and the text to bold.

7. Double click on the **Test message** to open it in its own window.

8. Close the **Test message** window by clicking the **Close** button, [✕], on the message's **Title Bar**.

Driving Lesson 17 - Flagging a Message

▣ Park and Read

A message can be **flagged** to indicate that further actions need to be carried out on it, such as follow up, call, reply, etc. The flag action can have a start date and a due date, and you can also choose to receive a reminder for it at a future date and time.

℞ Manoeuvres

1. Select a message in the **Inbox**, and then display the **Home** tab and click the **Follow Up** button, ▼ Follow Up ▾ , in the **Tags** group.

2. Select **Custom** from the list that appears.

ℹ️ *The same **Follow Up** button is also available from the **Ribbon** when a message is opened.*

3. Display the drop down list of **Flag to** reasons and select **Follow up**.

4. Leave the **Start date** as today's date but change the **Due date** to a future date and click **OK**. A coloured flag appears at the right of the message indicating a flag is set.

ℹ️ *To be reminded of a flagged action, you can tick the **Reminder** checkbox and set a date, time and sound effect to play.*

5. You can arrange flagged items in the **Message List** by start date and due date. Click **Arrange By** at the top of the list, Arrange By: Date (Conversations) , and select **Flag: Due Date**. Messages are now shown in the order they are due, with the soonest appearing first.

6. Click **Arrange By** again and select **Date** to restore the view.

7. Click the **Flag** icon on the message to mark it as complete. A tick appears in place of the flag.

8. To remove a flag, click the **Follow Up** button and select **Clear Flag** (or right click a flag icon and select **Clear Flag**). Remove the **Flag** just set by using either method.

ℹ️ *Flagged messages also appear on the **To-Do Bar** and in **Tasks**. If the **To-Do Bar** is minimised, only tasks that are due today will appear.*

Driving Lesson 18 - Attaching Files

▣ Park and Read

It is possible to attach any sort of file to an e-mail message in *Outlook,* provided it does not exceed any size/type restrictions imposed by the destination mailbox (if this is the case the message will be returned undelivered). This makes it easy to send reports, charts, sound files or pictures, for example. When the message reaches its destination, a paperclip icon, 📎, will let the recipient know there is an attachment.

Manoeuvres

1. Make sure the **Home** tab is selected and click the **New E-mail** button.

2. Enter your own e-mail address in the **To** box and enter the **Subject** as **Attachment**.

3. In the e-mail body, type the following text:

   Could you look at the attached file and let me know which wines you want to order for the party next week?

4. Click the **Attach File** button and the **Insert File** dialog box will appear.

5. Select the location where the data files are stored. Click the **Winelist** file to select it, and then click the **Insert** button.

6. The attachment appears in a new **Attached** box under the **Subject**.

ℹ *Depending on your default mail format settings, attachments may appear as icons in the e-mail body.*

7. To attach a second file, repeat steps **4** and **5**, this time double clicking the **Banking** file from the same location.

8. The **Banking** file has been attached in error. To delete this attachment, select its entry in the **Attached** box, and then press <**Delete**>.

9. Click **Send** to send the message together with its attachment, then if necessary **Send/Receive** on the **Send/Receive** tab to send the message.

ℹ *Outlook may warn you about sending messages with potentially unsafe attachments (files that are more likely to contain viruses). These include programs that have **.exe** extensions or scripts that have **.bat** extensions. Many mail servers will also reject e-mails with dangerous attachment types automatically, preventing your message from reaching its recipient.*

Driving Lesson 19 - Open and Save a File Attachment

P Park and Read

When a message with an attachment is received, it can be opened, saved, or both. You should be aware that some antivirus protection and firewall software can prevent you receiving certain types of attachment. If you are connected to a network – in an office for example – it may also have been set up to prevent access to these types of attachment. Typically, problems may occur when receiving files with an **.exe** or **.mdb** extension. These files run scripts and macros in order to function, as do many types of virus (attachments are a common way for viruses to be introduced to your system). Be *very* wary of opening any attachment if you are not absolutely sure of its source.

Manoeuvres

1. Create a new message and enter your own e-mail address in the **To** box. Enter the subject as **Saving Attachments**.

2. In the e-mail body, type: **The attached file may be of interest to you.**

3. Attach the **Maneaters** document from the data files, as described in the previous Driving Lesson.

4. Click **Send**, then if necessary **Send/Receive All Folders** on the **Send/Receive** tab to send the message.

5. As the message was addressed to you, after a few moments it will be displayed in the **Inbox** with an attachment icon. If it does not appear, you may need to click the **Send/Receive All Folders** button again.

Arrange By: Date	Newest on top ▼ ▲
◢ Today	
✉ Trainer	14:26
Saving Attachments	📎

ℹ️ *It is possible that Outlook will identify this message as **Junk Mail** and store it in a special **Junk E-mail** folder (if present). If so, open the **Junk E-mail** folder from the **Folder List** on the **Navigation Pane**, select the **Saving Attachments** message, click the **Junk** button, [Junk ▼], on the **Home** tab, and select **Not Junk**. The message will be moved to the **Inbox**.*

6. Make sure **Inbox** is selected on the **Navigation Pane** and double click on the **Saving Attachments** message to open it.

continued over

Driving Lesson 19 - Continued

7. To open the attachment, click on the **Maneaters** icon in the message. *Outlook* previews the document in the body of the e-mail.

Subject:	Saving Attachments
☑ Message	📄 Maneaters.docx (24 KB)

8. To open the attachment, select **Open** from the new **Attachments** tab on the **Ribbon** (or double click the **Maneaters** icon). Dismiss any warning messages that appear.

9. *Word* starts and displays the contents of the attached file.

ℹ *Microsoft Word 2010 may start in **Protected View**. As attachments are a common source of computer viruses, **Protected View** prevents them from making any changes to your computer.*

10. Close *Word* to return to *Outlook*.

11. To save the attachment without opening it, make sure the **Maneaters** icon is selected in the message window and click **Save As** on the **Attachments** tab.

12. When the **Save Attachment** dialog box is displayed, ensure that the save location is the data files folder.

Name	Date modified	Type
Banking.docx	03/06/2010 11:51	Microsoft
Kingtut.docx	03/06/2010 11:51	Microsoft
Letter1.docx	03/06/2010 11:51	Microsoft
Maneaters.docx	03/06/2010 11:51	Microsoft
Winelist.docx	03/06/2010 11:51	Microsoft

File name: Maneaters.docx
Save as type: Microsoft Word Document (*.docx)

13. Rename the **File name** to **Sharks.docx**.

14. Click **Save** to save the attached file, and then close the message window. The new file can now be found in the data files folder.

ℹ *Outlook will not automatically preview certain file types (such as **.exe** or **.bat** files) that are more likely to contain viruses.*

Driving Lesson 20 - Changing Message Importance

🅿 Park and Read

Messages have **Normal** priority by default, but it is possible to change their importance to either **High** or **Low**. This does not mean that they are sent more quickly or slowly, only that the recipient will be aware of their urgency by an icon on the message.

↱ Manoeuvres

1. Start a new message.

2. Address it to yourself and enter the subject as **Urgent!**

3. In the e-mail body, type: **Don't forget the meeting with the area manager at 2pm today.**

4. Make sure the **Message** tab is displayed on the **Ribbon** and click the **High Importance** button, ⚡ High Importance, from the **Tags** group.

5. Click **Send**, then if necessary **Send/Receive All Folders** on the **Send/Receive** tab to send the message.

6. When the message arrives in the **Inbox**, it will have an **Importance** icon set, ❗.

Arrange By: Date	Newest on top ▼ ▲
▲ Today	
✉ Trainer	13:30
Urgent!	❗

ℹ *The process to make a message low importance is the same. Select the **Low Importance** button from the **Ribbon** at step 4. A low importance icon, ⬇, will be shown when the message is received.*

Arrange By: Date	Newest on top ▼ ▲
▲ Today	
✉ Trainer	13:32
FYI	⬇

ℹ *Although less common, you can also set the sensitivity of a message to **Personal**, **Private** or **Confidential**. When creating a new e-mail, click the **Tags** group dialog box launcher, ▣, to display the **Properties** dialog box.*

Driving Lesson 21 - Reply to/Forward Messages

▣ Park and Read

A user can reply to the sender of a message, or to the original sender *and* all of the recipients. A reply can be entered into the e-mail body (the original message will be shown underneath for reference). A message can also be forwarded to another person.

↱ Manoeuvres

1. Within the **Inbox**, select the message named **Urgent** from the **Message List**.

2. Click on the **Reply** button in the **Respond** group to display a message window, addressed to the sender of the original e-mail. The original message is displayed underneath.

Reply

ℹ *The **Reply All** button is used to send a reply to all recipients of a message, if it was sent to more than one person.*

Reply All

3. If you never want the original message to appear in the replies you send, it can be omitted automatically. Close the reply message <u>without</u> saving and then display the **File** tab.

4. Click **Options** and select **Mail** from the categories list on the left. In the **Replies and forwards** section (you may need to scroll down to find this), open the drop down list **When replying to a message**.

5. Select **Do not include original message**.

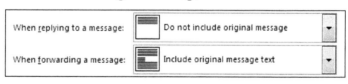

When replying to a message:	Do not include original message	▼
When forwarding a message:	Include original message text	▼

6. Click **OK**.

7. To see the effect of the new settings, make sure the **Urgent** message is selected in the **Message List** and click **Reply** again. Notice how the original message is not included.

8. The **Subject** section begins with **Re:** indicating a reply to a previous message. After **Re:**, delete the existing subject and replace it with **Replying to messages**.

9. Enter the following message text:

> **I was aware of the meeting. I should be there, but I'll let you know for sure soon.**

continued over

Driving Lesson 21 - Continued

10. Click **Send**, then if necessary **Send/Receive All Folders** on the **Send/Receive** tab to send the message.

11. To change the settings back to their original state, display the **File** tab and click **Options**. Select **Mail** from the list on the left and, in **Replies and forwards**, open the drop down list **When replying to a message**. Select **Include original message text** for the **replying** option.

| When replying to a message: | ≡ Include original message text | ▾ |
| When forwarding a message: | ≡ Include original message text | ▾ |

12. Click **OK** to confirm the change.

13. Select the **Urgent** message and click the **Reply** button in the **Respond** group. The original message is shown again but can be deleted manually – use the mouse to highlight the text, then delete it (this removes the original message from the current reply only).

14. Close the message window <u>without</u> saving.

15. Select the **Urgent** message once more, and then click the **Forward** button in the **Respond** group. When the message window is displayed, click in the **To** box and enter a friend's e-mail address.

16. The **Subject** begins with **FW:** indicating a forwarded message. Replace **Urgent!** with **Forwarding Messages**.

| Subject: | FW: Forwarding Messages |

17. A forwarding message can be typed in the e-mail body, leaving the original message underneath for reference. Enter the following text (above the original message):

> **This message is forwarded as part of Module 7 of the ECDL.**

18. Click **Send**, then if necessary **Send/Receive All Folders** on the **Send/Receive** tab to send the message. The message has been forwarded to a friend.

Driving Lesson 22 - Conversations

◪ Park and Read

Rather than show all of your e-mails in one large list, *Outlook* can gather messages with the same subject title into groups of related messages, known as a conversation thread.

⌒ Manoeuvres

1. Within the **Inbox**, select the message named **Urgent** from the **Message List**.

2. Click on the **Reply** button in the **Respond** group, and in the reply window that appears enter the following text above the original message:

    I can now confirm that I will be at the meeting, thank you.

3. Click **Send**, and then if necessary **Send/Receive All Folders** on the **Send/Receive** tab to send the message. As you are the original sender, the e-mail will be returned to you and will appear in the **Message List**.

4. Display the **View** tab and select **Show as Conversations** from the **Conversations** tab.

5. From the dialog that appears, select **This folder**. Messages within the **Inbox** *only* are now sorted by conversation; the **Urgent** message will appear grouped under the subject title **Urgent!**

Arrange By: Date (Conversations)	Newest on top ▲
◢ Today	
◢ Marketing	
◌ ✉	18:15
◌ Trainer	18:15
◌ Trainer	Thu 03/06 📎

ℹ *If only the latest message is shown, the conversation is minimised. Click the expand button, ▷, to view the entire thread.*

6. Click the first message in the group. The message is displayed in full on the **Reading Pane** (notice the original message below your reply).

ℹ *A large bullet to the left of a message indicates it is a new message in that conversation thread. All messages in the history of that conversation, including the e-mails you've sent, appear connected by smaller bullets.*

7. Click the **Show as Conversations** check box and select **This folder** again to return to the previous view.

Driving Lesson 23 - Contacts

🅿 Park and Read

To avoid having to remember the e-mail addresses of your contacts, known addresses can be stored by *Outlook* in an **Address Book**. If *Outlook* is being used on a network a **Global Address List** will also be available, listing the details and e-mail addresses of all users on the network. You can view your contacts in *Outlook* using the **Contacts** view.

🅿 Manoeuvres

1. Make sure the **Home** tab is selected and click the **Address Book** button, , to display the **Address Book**.

ℹ *The **Address Book** offers another view of your private **Contacts** list, but can be accessed from all other views in Outlook.*

2. The **Global Address List** may be displayed by default. It is usually not possible to add names to this list as it is automatically created and maintained by your server (and lists all users on your network). Click on the drop down arrow under **Address Book** and select **Contacts**.

🔲 Address Book: Contacts		⊟ ▣ ✕
File Edit Tools		
Search: ⦿ Name only ○ More columns **Address Book**		
[_____] Go Contacts - trainer@ciatraining.co.uk ▾	Advanced Find	
Name	Display Name	E-mail Address
Trainer	Trainer (trainer@ciatraining.co.uk)	trainer@ciatraining.co.uk

ℹ *There may be no **Contacts** records present if none have been added yet.*

3. From the **Address Book** window select **File | New Entry**. Select **New Contact** and click **OK**.

4. Enter your own details in the relevant boxes. There are many possible fields but only **Full Name** and **E-mail** are required for this guide. Click **Save & Close** to add the entry.

5. In the same way, add the names and details of **four** friends.

ℹ *A person in the **Global Address List** can be added to your private **Contacts** list by right clicking their name and selecting **Add to Contacts**.*

6. Close the **Address Book**.

Driving Lesson 24 - Add Sender to Contacts

▣ Park and Read

When a message is received from a contact, there is a quick and easy way to add that contact's details to your list of contacts.

⌒ Manoeuvres

1. Double click to open any message from your **Inbox** and right click on the **From** address.

2. Select **Add to Outlook Contacts** from the shortcut menu. When the contact window appears, add any further details that may be required, and then click **Save & Close**.

3. Close the message.

4. Open the **Address Book**, select **Contacts** and make sure you can see the new entry.

5. Close the **Address Book**.

6. The contact that was just added to has decided to move to a desert island, without leaving a forwarding address. Open the **Address Book** again and display your **Contacts**.

7. Select the new contact and press the <**Delete**> key. Click **Yes** at the prompt to delete the contact's details.

8. Close the **Address Book**.

Driving Lesson 25 - Contact Groups

🅿 Park and Read

It is possible to create **Contact Groups** of specific contacts, so that messages can be sent to groups of people with a single click of the mouse. Multiple contact groups (also known as distribution lists) can be created, each containing particular types of contact, such as family, darts team, friends, etc. Any contact can belong to more than one group.

Manoeuvres

1. To create a contact group from an existing address book, open the **Address Book**. Select **File | New Entry** and select **New Contact Group**.

2. Click **OK** to display the **Untitled – Contact Group** window.

3. Enter **Friends** in the **Name** box. This will be the name of the new contact group.

4. Click **Add Members** from the **Members** group and select **From Outlook Contacts**.

5. Select a name from the list and click the **Members** button at the bottom of the dialog box. That contact is added to the list of group members shown.

Select Members: Contacts			
Search: ⦿ Name only ○ More columns		**Address Book**	
[ ] Go		Contacts - trainer@ciatraining.co.uk ▾	Advanced Find

Name	Display Name	E-mail Address
👤 Darren Stokes	Darren Stokes (dstokes@stokesconsultant.co.uk)	dstokes@stokesconsultant.co.uk
👤 David Lyon	David Lyon (dave@lyonsaa.co.uk)	dave@lyonsaa.co.uk
👤 Rav Patel	Rav Patel (rav@ironworks.net)	rav@ironworks.net
👤 Trainer	Trainer (trainer@ciatraining.co.uk)	trainer@ciatraining.co.uk

Members Button → Members ->   Darren Stokes (dstokes@stokesconsultant.co.uk);

OK   Cancel

ℹ️ *You can select more than one contact at a time by pressing and holding <Ctrl> and clicking each item. Then, click the **Members** button to add all the selected contacts to the contact list in one go.*

6. Repeat the process to add two other friends to the list.

continued over

Driving Lesson 25 - Continued

7.   Click **OK** to return to the **Friends – Contact Group** window.

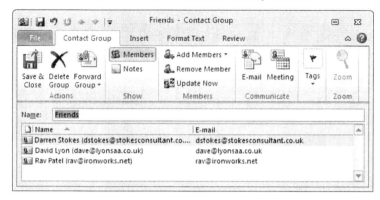

i *Notice there is also a button on the **Ribbon** to remove members from the group. Removing a member does not delete them from your contacts.*

8.   Click **Save & Close**. The **Friends** contact group is added to the **Address Book**.

👤 David Lyon	David Lyon (dave@lyonsaa.co.uk)
👥 **Friends**	**Friends**
👤 Rav Patel	Rav Patel (rav@ironworks.net)

9.   Close the **Address Book** and compose a new message.

10.   To send the message to everyone in the new **Friends** contact group, click the **To** button to show your **Address Book** again. Display your **Contacts** list and the **Friends** group appears alongside your other contacts.

11.   Select **Friends** from the list and click **To** to add it as the target address, and then click **OK**. The group name is added to the message, and the message will be sent to all addresses included in the **Friends** contact group.

12.   The message will be sent to all addresses included in the **Friends** contact group. Enter the subject as **Contact Groups**.

13.   Type in a suitable message and send it.

i *Once the message is sent, all the individual addresses in the contact group will be shown in the **To** address box.*

i *To send the same message to several people in the **Address Book** who are not in a contact group, click the **To** button,* To... *, then double click on each required name, before clicking **OK**.*

Driving Lesson 26 - Revision

This covers the features introduced in this section. Try not to refer to the preceding Driving Lessons while completing it.

1. Check for any new messages in the **Inbox**.

2. Read any that may have arrived.

3. Select any single message that has been read and mark it as unread.

4. Flag the selected message.

5. Remove the flag.

6. Close any open messages.

7. Open **Contacts** in your **Address Book** and add three new entries, using the names and addresses of colleagues.

8. Create a new contact group in **Contacts**, named **Colleagues**, and add the new entries to it.

9. Create a new message and address it to the **Colleagues** contact group, and enter the subject as **Letter Draft**.

10. Attach the file **Letter1** located in the data files folder.

11. Enter the message text as follows:

   Here is the first draft of my letter. What do you think?

12. Make the message **High Importance**.

13. Send the message.

If you experienced any difficulty completing the Revision, refer back to the Driving Lessons in this section. Then redo the Revision.

Driving Lesson 27 - Revision

This covers the features introduced in this section. Try not to refer to the preceding Driving Lessons while completing it.

1. Start a new message and address it to yourself.

2. Copy in, or **Cc**, a friend or colleague.

3. Enter the **Subject** as **Results**.

4. Attach the file **League** located in the data files folder.

5. Enter the body of the message as: **Here are those hockey results you wanted**.

6. Send the message.

7. When the **Results** message arrives back save the attachment in your **Documents** folder.

If you experienced any difficulty completing the Revision, refer back to the Driving Lessons in this section. Then redo the Revision.

Driving Lesson 28 - Revision

This covers the features introduced in this section. Try not to refer to the preceding Driving Lessons while completing it.

1.   Create a contact group named **Staff**.

2.   Add three friends or colleagues to the list.

3.   Create a new message.

4.   Address the message to the **Staff** contact group.

5.   Send a carbon copy to yourself.

6.   Enter the **Subject** as **Team Building Trip**.

7.   Make the message high importance.

8.   Enter the following message:

> **This month's outing is to a local paint balling range. Please let me know if you are free on Friday week.**

9.   Send the message.

10. When you receive the **Team Building Trip** message, flag it.

11. Reply to the message, saying that you are free.

12. Send the message.

If you experienced any difficulty completing the Revision, refer back to the Driving Lessons in this section. Then redo the Revision.

Once you are confident with the features, complete the Record of Achievement Matrix referring to the section at the end of the guide. Only when competent move on to the next Section.

Section 4
Message
Management

By the end of this Section you should be able to:

Save a Draft Message

Print Messages

Delete Messages

Organise Messages in Folders

To gain an understanding of the above features, work through the **Driving Lessons** in this **Section**.

For each **Driving Lesson**, read the **Park and Read** instructions, without touching the keyboard, then work through the numbered steps of the **Manoeuvres** on the computer. Complete the **Revision Exercise(s)** at the end of the section to test your knowledge.

Driving Lesson 29 - Save a Draft Message

P Park and Read

Occasionally, you may be in the middle of typing a message when you have to leave it, perhaps to check information. This doesn't mean the message is lost - you can save a draft copy and come back to it later.

Manoeuvres

1.   With **Inbox** selected in the **Folders List**, start a new e-mail with the subject **Meeting**.

2.   Enter your own e-mail address in the **To** box.

3.   Type in the message: **Are you available for the staffing meeting on**.

4.   You need to check the date of the meeting. Click the **Close** button on the message window, ⊠. The following prompt appears:

5.   Click **Yes**. The message is saved in the **Drafts** folder (the **Drafts** folder will be created if one does not exist already).

i   *Alternatively, to save to **Drafts** manually, display the **File** tab and then select **Save**, click **Save** on the **Quick Access Toolbar**, or simply press <**Ctrl S**>.*

6.   Select **Drafts**, 📑 Drafts [1], from the **Folders List** on the **Navigation Pane**. There should be at least one item in the **Message List** – the **Meeting** draft.

7.   Double click on the message to open it. You can now continue the e-mail from where you left it.

8.   Close the message. If you are prompted to save again, click **No**.

9.   Delete the message from the **Drafts** folder and leave *Outlook* open.

Driving Lesson 30 - Printing a Message

▣ Park and Read

Messages can be printed by simply opening the desired e-mail, and then selecting the print command. The number of copies and print range can be selected as required.

↰ Manoeuvres

1. Within your **Inbox**, select any message from the **Message List** but do <u>not</u> open it.

2. Display the **File** tab and click **Print** (or simply press **<Ctrl P>**). The **Print** screen is displayed.

> **Print**
>
> Specify how you want the item to be printed and then click Print.
>
> Print
>
> **Printer**   ⓘ
>
> HP LaserJet P2015 Series PCL 6 on BASSWOOD.companyn... ▾
> Ready
>
> 🖨 Print Options
>
> **Settings**
>
> ▦ Table Style
>
> ▤ Memo Style

ℹ️ *A **Preview** of the message as it will be printed is automatically shown on the preview panel.*

3. Select a printer from the **Printer** drop down list (your default printer, if available, will be automatically selected).

4. Make sure **Memo Style** is selected under **Settings**.

ℹ️ *Table Style prints a list of items in your mailbox.*

5. Click the **Print** button to print a single copy of the e-mail on your selected printer and to automatically return to your mailbox.

continued over

Driving Lesson 30 - Continued

6.   To print more than one copy of an e-mail, again display the **File** tab and click **Print**.

7.   Click the **Print Options** button, 🖶 Print Options. A **Print** dialog box appears.

Print

Printer

Name: \\BASSWOOD\HP LaserJet P2015 Series PCL 6   [▼]   [Properties]

Status:
Type: HP LaserJet P2015 Series PCL 6
Where: ☐ Print to file
Comment:

Print style   Copies

▦ Table Style   [Page Setup...]   Number of pages: [All ▼]

▤ Memo Style   Number of copies: [1]

                          [Define Styles..]   ☐ Collate copies

Page range

◉ All

☐ Pages: [   ]

Type page numbers and/or page ranges separated by commas counting from the start of the item. For example, type 1, 3 or 5-12.

Print options

☐ Print attached files. Attachments will print to the default printer only.

                                [Print]   [Preview]   [Cancel]

8.   In **Number of copies** (within the **Copies** group), use the up spinner to increase the number to **2**.

ℹ️ *To only print specific pages rather than the entire message, enter the desired page numbers (or range of page number, e.g. 2-3) in the **Pages** box.*

ℹ️ *You can also choose to print all attached files in addition to the message. To do this, select **Print attached files** in the **Print options** group.*

ℹ️ *When previewing an attachment, you can print it directly to your default printer using the **Quick Print** button on the **Attachments** tab.*

🖨️ Quick Print

9.   Select a printer from the **Name** drop down list, and then click **Print** to print two copies of the e-mail. You will automatically return to your mailbox.

Driving Lesson 31 - Deleting Messages

▣ Park and Read

All messages received are stored in the **Inbox**. After a period of time you will probably want to remove old, redundant messages. Once selected, messages can be deleted and are moved from the **Inbox** to the **Deleted Items** folder, a temporary store, until confirmation of permanent deletion.

↱ Manoeuvres

1. With the **Inbox** selected, select the **Test message** you created earlier from the **Message List**.

2. Make sure the **Home** tab is displayed, and then click the **Delete** button. The **Test message** e-mail is deleted from the **Inbox**.

> ℹ️ *To select all messages, press <**Ctrl A**>; to select non adjacent messages hold the <**Ctrl**> key and click the required messages; to select a range, use the <**Shift**> key and click the first and last messages.*

3. Select **Deleted Items** from the **Folders List** on the **Navigation Pane**, 📄 Deleted Items (6) . The **Message List** will now show all deleted messages (including **Test message**).

4. To retrieve the **Test message** and restore it to the **Inbox**, select it and then click **Move** on the **Ribbon**. From the list that appears, select **Inbox**.

5. View the **Inbox** folder to see that the message has been restored.

> ℹ️ *A deleted message can also be clicked and dragged from where it is being viewed in the **Deleted Items** folder to the required folder in the **Folders List**.*

6. Delete the message again, but this time use the <**Delete**> key (which is an alternative method of deletion).

7. View the **Deleted Items** folder; the message has reappeared.

8. To empty the **Deleted Items** folder, display the **Folder** tab and click the **Empty Folder** button in the **Clean Up** group.

9. On the warning message box, select **Yes** and any deleted messages will be permanently deleted.

> ℹ️ *The useful **Clean Up Folder** button, also in the **Clean Up** group, can be used to automatically delete redundant e-mails from your mailbox. Messages that are old or have not been accessed in a long time will be removed and placed in the **Deleted Items** folder. Unread or flagged messages will not be affected.*

Driving Lesson 32 - Creating Folders

🅿 Park and Read

To help organise your mailbox, it may be a good idea to create a system of folders in which to store your messages (this is particularly useful for filing messages from certain people or on a specific subject). Once folders have been set up, messages can be sent directly to them on receipt. Messages can be moved between folders as required, and unwanted folders can be easily deleted.

☞ Manoeuvres

1. To create your own mail folder within the **Inbox**, first make sure the **Inbox** is selected in the **Folders List**. Display the **Folder** tab and click the **New Folder** button in the **New** group to display the **Create New Folder** dialog.

2. In the **Name** box, type your first name and click **OK**. The new folder has been created.

3. The **Navigation Pane** changes to show the new folder underneath **Inbox**. If the structure within **Inbox** is hidden, expand it by clicking the arrow to the left, ▷🗀 **Inbox** (1).

ℹ️ *Folders can be created within any of the displayed folders. To delete a selected folder, display the **Folder** tab and click **Delete Folder** in the **Actions** group.*

Driving Lesson 33 - Organising Messages

▣ Park and Read

Once folders have been created in your mailbox, messages can be moved between them if necessary.

↱ Manoeuvres

1. Make sure the **Inbox** folder is selected in the **Folders List**.

2. Select any message from the **Message List**. You are going to move this message to the folder you created earlier.

3. Display the **Home** tab, and click the **Move** button, [⤷ Move ▾], in the **Move** group. Select the folder name that you created in the previous driving lesson.

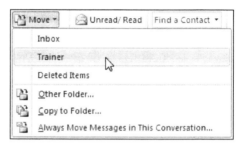

4. The message has been moved. Open your folder to check.

ℹ️ *Messages can also be moved in the **Message List** by clicking and dragging them to another folder in the **Folders List**.*

5. Click and drag the message from your folder back to the **Inbox** folder.

Driving Lesson 34 - Creating Rules

Park and Read

Rules can be created in *Outlook* to automatically perform actions when certain messages are received (or sent). For example, messages on a particular subject can be automatically moved to a specific folder, or messages from certain people can create an alert.

Manoeuvres

1. Make sure the **Inbox** is selected and the **Home** tab is displayed. Select any message from the **Message List** that you sent to yourself.

2. To create a rule based on the selected message (which is easier than creating a new rule from scratch), click the **Rules** button, [Rules ▾], in the **Move** group and then select **Create Rule**.

3. To instruct *Outlook* to move all incoming mail with the word "ECDL" in the subject to a specific folder, check the **Subject contains** option and replace the text with **ECDL**.

4. Check the **Move the item to folder** option. Find the folder you created earlier in this guide (with your first name) and click **OK**. You may need to expand **Inbox** to see it.

5. Click **OK** again. A dialog appears confirming that the rule **ECDL** has been created successfully. Click **OK** once more to activate the rule.

ℹ️ *Many more rule conditions and actions can be applied by clicking the* ***Advanced Options*** *button on the* ***Create Rule*** *dialog box.*

continued over

Driving Lesson 34 - Continued

6. From now on, all e-mail addressed to you with the word **ECDL** in the subject will be automatically placed in your new folder, not the **Inbox**.

7. Test the rule by sending yourself a message with the subject: **This ECDL guide is excellent!**

i *You can also apply new rules to items __already__ in your mailbox by clicking the* ***Run Rules Now*** *button in the* ***Clean Up*** *group on the* ***Folder*** *tab.*

8. To remove a rule, make sure the **Inbox** and **Home** tab is displayed and click the **Rules** button again. Select **Manage Rules & Alerts**.

9. A list of rules appears in the **E-mail Rules** tab. Select the rule you just created (called **ECDL**) and click **Delete**. Click **Yes** to confirm then click **OK** to close the dialog box. The rule will no longer affect your mailbox.

10. To delete your new folder, select it on the **Folders List** and press <**Delete**> (or click **Delete Folder** on the **Folder** tab).

11. A confirmation box is displayed. Click **Yes** to delete the folder.

i *The deleted folder and its contents are moved to the* ***Deleted Items*** *folder. To remove the folder permanently, expand* ***Deleted Items*** *to show your folder and press* <***Delete***> *again.*

Driving Lesson 35 - Finding Messages

▣ Park and Read

It is possible to search for messages in various ways. For example, you can search for messages from a particular person, with a specific subject, or containing certain content.

🖝 Manoeuvres

1. Make sure **Inbox** is selected and locate the **Search** box at the top of the **Message List** (or press **<Ctrl E>**).

Search Inbox (Ctrl+E)	🔍
Arrange By: Date	Newest on top ▼ ▲

ℹ️ *Notice that the **Search** tab appears on the **Ribbon**.*

2. Type **attachment** in the **Search** box, `attachment ✕`. As the word is being entered the **Inbox** will be searched for messages which contain the text.

attachm	✕
Arrange By: Date	Newest on top ▼ ▲

   ◢ Today

✉ Trainer	14:36
Saving Attachments	📎
✉ Trainer	14:36
Attachment	📎

   Did you find what you were searching for?

   Try searching again in All Mail Items.

ℹ️ *The default search option is to search <u>all</u> of the text in the messages for a match, so the above example would find any messages where the search word appears in the **Subject**, the **Body** of the message or the **To** and **From** fields.*

3. Click the close button, `✕`, on the **Search** box to clear the search and display all messages again.

4. To search for items by **Importance**, click in the **Search** box again (or press **<Ctrl E>**). Click the **Important** button in the Refine group to show all messages that have high importance. Click the **Important** button again to clear the search.

5. Click **Flagged** to search for items with a flag set. Click the **Flagged** button again to clear.

continued over

Driving Lesson 35 - Continued

6.   Click **Has Attachments** to search for items with an attachment. Click the **Has Attachments** button again to clear.

[i] *You can use the refine buttons on the **Search** tab in any order or combination.*

7.   Click the **Subject** button in the **Refine** group and type **Sending**. The text will appear in the **Search** box between brackets.

subject:(Sending		×
Arrange By: Date	Newest on top	

8.   Any message with "sending" in the **Subject** field will now be displayed. Messages with the text "sending" in the body of the message will not be shown.

[i] *By default, Outlook searches through messages in the currently selected folder (e.g. **Inbox**). To search all folders in your mailbox, select **All Mail Items** in the **Scope** group.*

[i] *You can search for messages by **sender** in a similar way by clicking the **From** button in the **Refine** group.*

9.   Click the **Close Search** button in the **Close** group to clear the search and display all messages again.

[i] *The **Close Search** button has the same effect as clicking the ⊠ button in the **Search** box.*

[i] *For more complex searches, click the **Search Tools** button in the **Options** group of the **Search** tab and select **Advanced Find**.*

Driving Lesson 36 - Revision

This covers the features introduced in this section. Try not to refer to the preceding Driving Lessons while completing it.

1. Print three copies of any message in your **Inbox**.

2. Organise all messages in your **Inbox** by **Subject** in ascending alphabetical order.

3. Print the first message in the list.

4. Search for any messages in the **Inbox** with the message text containing the word **team**.

5. Search for any messages with attachments.

6. Search for any messages that have been flagged.

7. Search for any messages received from yourself.

8. Create a new folder in the **Inbox**, called **ECDL Module 7**.

9. Move all of the messages created during this module into the new folder.

10. Sort the messages by date received, with the most recent at the top of the list.

11. Delete the **ECDL Module 7** folder and all of its contents.

12. Empty the **Deleted Items** folder.

13. Close *Outlook*.

i *You can now safely delete any contacts, distribution lists or e-mails created during this guide.*

If you experienced any difficulty completing the Revision, refer back to the Driving Lessons in this section. Then redo the Revision.

Once you are confident with the features, complete the Record of Achievement Matrix referring to the section at the end of the guide.

Answers

Driving Lesson 7

Step 1   E-mail is beneficial for businesses because it is very fast, cheap and web based accounts can be accessed from any computer with Internet access.

Step 2   **Netiquette** is network etiquette: a set of rules governing how you should use e-mail.

Step 3   Messages may contain viruses.

Step 4   Make sure you have up to date anti-virus software installed. Save attachments and scan them before opening if you are suspicious.

Step 5   E-mail is electronic mail.

Step 6   An e-mail address consists of a **user name**, an **@ sign** and a **domain name**.

Glossary

Attachment	Any file transmitted with an e-mail.
BCC	Blind Carbon Copy.
CC	Carbon Copy.
Contact Group	A grouping of several mail addresses than can be accessed with a single name. Also known as a distribution list.
Conversation	A way for organising your mailbox by conversation thread.
Column	Message information can be shown and sorted in columns.
E-mail	Electronic Mail.
Folder	A method of grouping together files (and other folders).
Forward (a message)	Send a copy of an e-mail which you have received, to another address, with an optional message of your own.
Inbox	The default folder for storing all incoming e-mail messages.
Mail Rules	Definable rules on how to treat incoming e-mails depending on certain conditions.
Message List	A list of all messages in the current mailbox folder.
Navigation Pane	A panel of buttons and folders used to activate the various features of *Outlook*.
Netiquette	Network etiquette: a set of rules governing how you should use e-mail.
Outbox	The folder for storing outgoing e-mails before they have been sent.
Reading Pane	A view where the contents of messages can be previewed without opening them.
Ribbon	A collections of tab bars containing groups of related features. Found in all *Office 2010* applications.
Sent Items	The folder for storing copies of e-mails after they have been sent.
Subfolder	A folder that is contained within another folder.

Index

Record of Achievement Matrix

This Matrix is to be used to measure your progress while working through the guide. This is a learning reinforcement process, you judge when you are competent.

Tick boxes are provided for each feature. 1 is for no knowledge, 2 some knowledge and 3 is for competent. A section is only complete when column 3 is completed for all parts of the section.

For details on sitting ECDL Examinations in your country please contact the local ECDL Licensee or visit the European Computer Driving Licence Foundation Limited web site at http://www.ecdl.com.

Tick the Relevant Boxes **1**: No Knowledge   **2**: Some Knowledge   **3**: Competent

Section	No	Driving Lesson	1	2	3
1 Outlook	1	Using E-mail			
	2	Using Outlook			
	3	E-mail Help			
	4	Views			
	5	Sorting Messages			
	6	Closing Outlook			
2 Message Editing	8	Creating a Message			
	9	Cut, Copy and Paste Messages			
	10	Cut, Copy and Paste from Word			
	11	Spell Checker			
	12	Applying a Signature			
3 Send and Receive	15	Sending Messages			
	16	Open and Read Messages			
	17	Flagging a Message			
	18	Attaching Files			
	19	Open and Save a File Attachment			
	20	Changing Message Importance			
	21	Reply to/Forward Messages			
	22	Conversations			
	23	Contacts			
	24	Add Sender to Contacts			
	25	Contact Groups			
4 Message Management	29	Save a Draft Message			
	30	Printing a Message			
	31	Deleting Messages			
	32	Creating Folders			
	33	Organising Messages			
	34	Creating Rules			
	35	Finding Messages			

Other Products from CiA Training

CiA Training is a leading publishing company which has consistently delivered the highest quality products since 1985. Our experienced in-house publishing team has developed a wide range of flexible and easy to use self-teach resources for individual learners and corporate clients all over the world.

At the time of publication, we currently offer approved ECDL materials for:

- **ECDL Syllabus 5.0**

- **ECDL Syllabus 5.0 Revision Series**

- **ECDL Advanced Syllabus 2.0**

- **ECDL Advanced Syllabus 2.0 Revision Series**

Previous syllabus versions are also available upon request.

We hope you have enjoyed using this guide and would love to hear your opinions about our materials. To let us know how we're doing, and to get up to the minute information on our current range of products, please visit us at:

www.ciatraining.co.uk